Geothermal Energy

Using Earth's Furnace

Carrie Gleason

Crabtree Publishing Company
www.crabtreebooks.com

Crabtree Publishing Company

www.crabtreebooks.com

Author: Carrie Gleason
Coordinating editor: Chester Fisher
Project Manager: Kavita Lad (Q2AMEDIA)
Art direction: Rahul Dhiman (Q2AMEDIA)
Design: Ranjan Singh (Q2AMEDIA)
Photo research: Akansha Srivastava (Q2AMEDIA)
Editor: Ellen Roger
Copy editor: Mike Hodge
Project editor: Robert Walker
Production coordinator: Katherine Kantor
Prepress technician: Katherine Kantor

Photographs: P3: Corbis (bottom left), Istockphoto (bottom right); P4: Stephan Hoerold / Istockphoto; P5: US Geological Survey; P6: Shell Photographic Services, Shell International Ltd; P7: Photolibrary; P9 a, b, c, d: Shutterstock; P11: Tony Waltham / Photolibrary; P12: Frans Lemmens / Lonely Planet Images; P13: Kobi Israel / Photolibrary; P15: Patrick Endres / Alaskastock.com; P18: Graham Prentice / Shutterstock; P19: Steven R. Brantley / USGS Volcano Hazards Team; P20: JTB Photo / Photolibrary; P21: Jack Birns / Stringer / Getty Images; P22: Phillip Norton; P23: Associated Press (top); P24: Vance Smith/Istockphoto; P25: Jaroslav Pap / Associated Press; P26: Philippe Plailly / Eurelios / Science Photo Library; P29: Steve Finn / Staff / Getty Images; P30: Juliet Coombe / Lonely Planet Images (top); P30: Westend 61 / Alamy (bottom); P31: Laurence Gough / Shutterstock.

Cover: Kim Hart/ Robert Harding Travel/Photolibrary
Blue lagoon; Svarsengi geothermal plant, Iceland.

Title page: Yellowstone National Park
Constant geyser erupting; Norris Geyser Basin, Yellowstone National Park.

Library and Archives Canada Cataloguing in Publication

Gleason, Carrie, 1973-
    Geothermal energy : using earth's furnace / Carrie Gleason.

(Energy revolution)
Includes index.
ISBN 978-0-7787-2917-4 (bound).
--ISBN 978-0-7787-2931-0 (pbk.)

    1. Geothermal resources--Juvenile literature. 2. Geothermal engineering--Juvenile literature. I. Title. II. Series.

TJ280.7.G54 2008   j333.8'8   C2008-901525-8

Library of Congress Cataloging-in-Publication Data

Gleason, Carrie, 1973-
    Geothermal energy : using earth's furnace / Carrie Gleason.
        p. cm. -- (Energy revolution)

Includes index.
    ISBN-13: 978-0-7787-2931-0 (pbk. : alk. paper)
    ISBN-10: 0-7787-2931-1 (pbk. : alk. paper)
    ISBN-13: 978-0-7787-2917-4 (reinforced library binding : alk. paper)
    ISBN-10: 0-7787-2917-6 (reinforced library binding : alk. paper)
    1. Geothermal resources--Juvenile literature. I. Title. II. Series.

GB1199.5.G58 2008
621.44--dc22
                                    2008012079

Crabtree Publishing Company

www.crabtreebooks.com   1-800-387-7650

Published in Canada
Crabtree Publishing
616 Welland Ave.
St. Catharines, ON
L2M 5V6

Published in the United States
Crabtree Publishing
PMB16A
350 Fifth Ave., Suite 3308
New York, NY 10118

Published in the United Kingdom
Crabtree Publishing
White Cross Mills
High Town, Lancaster
LA1 4XS

Published in Australia
Crabtree Publishing
386 Mt. Alexander Rd.
Ascot Vale (Melbourne)
VIC 3032

Contents

Energy Conservation: "We Can Do It!"

"We Can Do It" was a slogan that appeared on posters made during World War II. One poster featured "Rosie the Riveter," a woman dressed in blue coveralls (shown below). The poster was originally intended to encourage women to enter the workforce in industry to replace the men who left to serve in the war. Today, the image of Rosie the Riveter represents a time when people came together as a society to reach a common goal. Today's energy challenge can be combatted in a similar way. Together, we can work to save our planet from the pollution caused by burning fossil fuels by learning to conserve energy and developing alternative energy sources.

Energy

In a world without *energy*, there would be no movement, no light, and no life. Everything would be dark and still. Energy makes things happen.

What is Energy?

People use the word energy in many ways. When people talk of how lively they feel, they often say they "have a lot of energy." Newspapers write about an energy crisis or about energy **consumption**. Even advertisements for appliances sometimes boast that their products are **energy efficient**. According to scientists, energy is the amount of **work** something can do.

Power Up

Energy can be changed into different forms, but it cannot be created or destroyed. Electrical energy, or electricity, is one form of energy. It is used to heat our homes and run our lights and appliances. Sometimes, the words "energy" and "power" are used for the same thing, but energy and power are not the same. Power is the rate at which energy is used. It is measured in watts, or joules per second. Written on a light bulb, for example, is 40, 60, or 100 watts. These numbers mean that the light bulb uses 40, 60, or 100 joules of energy per second. Usually, electricity supplies this energy.

Everything we do, including riding a bike, requires energy. People get energy from the food they eat.

Energy from Food

We need energy to stay alive! The food we eat contains energy. When we eat, our bodies **metabolize** food, or convert food into usable energy. We use this energy to breathe, move, and think. We even use energy when we are sleeping. The amount of food we eat and the kinds of food we eat influences the amount of energy in our bodies.

A volcano releases energy equivalent to several nuclear bombs. If harnessed properly, this energy could be a very cheap means to generate power.

Forms of Energy

Energy can be stored. Energy is stored in food. It is also stored in batteries. Energy can also be moving energy. An example of moving energy is wind. Heat is also a form of moving energy, called thermal energy. Forms of moving energy include wind, heat, the sun's rays, and lightning. Forms of stored energy include **biomass** and fossil fuels.

Solar energy

Wind energy

Electrical energy

Heat energy

Conservation Tip

Energy conservation means reducing the amount of power that we use. You can find tips on how to conserve energy and facts about energy conservation in boxes like these.

Fueling Today

Today, countries around the world are realizing that their energy-consumption habits, or how much energy they use, is harming Earth. Fossil fuels are the main energy source used worldwide. Oil, natural gas, and coal are fossil fuels. When these energy sources are burned in power plants, factories, cars, or other forms of transportation, they create **emissions**, or waste gases. Most scientists say these emissions damage the **environment**.

Energy Sources

An energy source is anything that contains energy. Energy sources are either renewable or non-renewable. Renewable sources can be **replenished** by nature. Examples of renewable energy sources are solar energy, wind energy, and biomass. Non-renewable energy sources cannot quickly be replenished. Coal, oil, and natural gas are non-renewable sources, so today's main energy sources will one day run out.

Energy Dependence

Most countries depend on fossil fuels. Each day, ships, railroad cars, and pipelines move huge amounts of fossil fuels around the world to where they are needed. Worldwide, oil provides 95 percent of the energy needed for transportation, and 40 percent of all electricity comes from burning coal in power plants. Not all countries have their own supply of oil, coal, or natural gas. Many have to import, or buy it, from other countries. This situation makes them dependent on foreign supplies. The United States, for example, has to import about half of the 20 million barrels of oil it uses each day. Japan and Iceland have to import all of their fossil fuels. They have few **reserves** of their own.

Fossil fuels were created hundreds of millions of years ago from the remains of dead plants and animals.

Global Warming

Layers of gases called the **atmosphere** trap the sun's heat and keep Earth warm. Nitrogen, oxygen, and carbon dioxide gases exist naturally in the atmosphere. When fossil fuels are burned, they release waste gases, including carbon dioxide. This carbon dioxide adds to the amount of gas that is already in the atmosphere. As a result, too much heat from the sun is trapped next to Earth, and the planet's temperature is rising. Scientists call this effect global warming. The long-term effects of global warming are not yet known. Many scientists believe, however, that it may lead to more severe storms and flooding of coastal areas.

In North America, we depend on fossil fuels to provide transportation and to create electricity. Most of the technology we use today, from automobiles to airplanes, was built to run on fossil fuels. Carbon dioxide is released when fossil fuels are burned. It is believed to be a major contributor to global warming.

Earth's Heat

Geothermal energy is one source of energy that is renewable and can replace some of the fossil fuels used today. Geothermal means Earth's heat. This heat energy comes from deep inside the planet.

There are seven continents on Earth. The continents are Asia, Africa, North America, South America, Australia, Europe, and Antarctica. Five oceans—the Pacific Ocean, Atlantic Ocean, Indian Ocean, Southern Ocean, and Arctic Ocean—flow around the continents.

Deep-Down Heat

More than 3,870 miles (6,228 km) down toward the center of Earth, the temperature may reach an incredibly hot 7,000°F (3,870°C). Some of this heat is left over from when Earth formed over four billion years ago. Heat is also continually produced deep within Earth by the decay of **radioactive** particles, or pieces, of rock. Over time, the heat slowly makes its way to the surface. This heat is called geothermal energy. It is increasingly being seen as a cheap, renewable source of power.

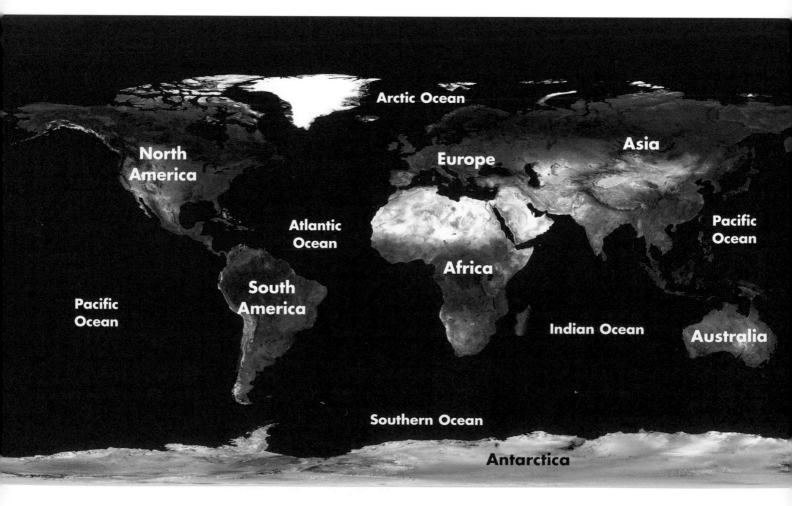

Earth's Layers

Earth is divided into layers. At the center of Earth is a solid inner **core** that scientists believe is about the size of the moon. It is made up mostly of iron. A liquid outer core surrounds the inner core. Around the outer core is the **mantle**. The mantle is made up of rock, some of which has been melted by the heat from the core. The outermost layer of Earth, the layer we live on, is called the **crust**. Compared to the other layers, the crust is thin. It is made up of mostly dirt and rock. The oceans and the continents sit on the crust.

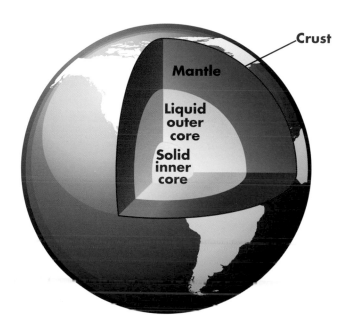

Crust

Mantle

Liquid outer core

Solid inner core

Moving the Heat

Magma is the carrier that moves Earth's heat to the surface. Magma is melted rock in the mantle layer. It is less dense, or lighter, than the solid rock of the mantle, so it moves in a process called **convection** toward Earth's crust. In some places, mostly volcanoes, magma pushes up through Earth's crust. When magma reaches the surface, it is called **lava**. Erupting volcanoes are an example of geothermal activity.

Green, Clean Energy

Using geothermal energy does less damage to the environment than using fossil fuels does. Geothermal energy is known as a green, or clean, energy source. Below is a list of other energy sources that are green and renewable.

- The energy found in wind can be used to generate electricity by driving a turbine.

- Solar energy is the energy from the sun. Solar panels absorb the sun's energy to make electricity.

- Hydropower uses the energy of rushing water to create electricity.

- Biomass includes all organisms on Earth and their waste. Grasses, trees, plants, animal manure, and sewage are all forms of biomass used for energy. Biomass stores the sun's energy. When biomass is burned, the sun's energy is released.

Hot Rocks, Hot Water

Most magma stays below Earth's surface. It flows deep under ground, heating rocks and underground pools of water called reservoirs. When magma heats water, the water becomes the carrier of geothermal energy to the surface. Sometimes, a column of water that has been heated to **water vapor**, or steam, shoots out of a crack on Earth's surface. These columns are called **geysers**. There are few geysers on Earth, and most are clumped together in geyser fields. Geysers are most commonly found in Iceland, New Zealand, and the United States.

Geothermal Energy

Geothermal energy comes to Earth's surface in other ways, too. **Hot springs** occur where hot water from geothermal reservoirs seeps to the surface and collects in pools. Hot springs are found all over the world. **Mudpots** are areas of bubbling mud formed when hot water seeps through rock and soaks into **silt** and clay.

Geysers form when hot water and cold water mix under ground. When the water boils, it creates pressure and erupts as a shooting column of steam. Yellowstone National Park in Wyoming contains about 500 geysers. There are also geysers in Alaska, Nevada, California, and Oregon.

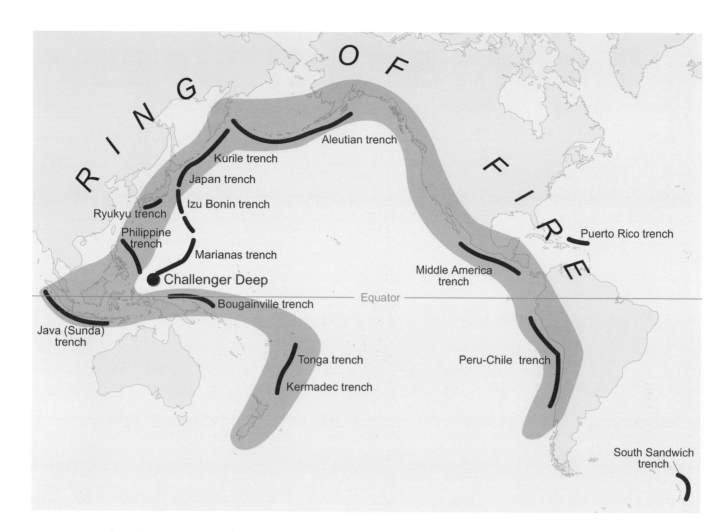

The map shows the Ring of Fire with the following trenches labeled: Aleutian trench, Kurile trench, Japan trench, Izu Bonin trench, Ryukyu trench, Philippine trench, Marianas trench, Challenger Deep, Bougainville trench, Java (Sunda) trench, Tonga trench, Kermadec trench, Middle America trench, Puerto Rico trench, Peru-Chile trench, South Sandwich trench, Equator.

Around the World

Earth's crust is made up of large pieces called **plates**. They fit together like a jigsaw puzzle. The plates are floating on magma. The best places to tap into geothermal energy are the areas where magma is close to the surface, such as where two plates meet. The Ring of Fire is one such place. The Ring of Fire is an area along the edges of the Pacific Ocean where most of the world's active volcanoes are found. Magma is also close to the surface where the plates are separating. Examples of these areas are Iceland, the Great Rift Valley in Africa, and the southwestern United States. The countries that currently use the most geothermal energy are the United States, New Zealand, Italy, Iceland, Mexico, the Philippines, Indonesia, and Japan.

The Pacific Ocean has the maximum number of active volcanoes, forming a fiery ring around its edges.

Conservation Tip

Prevent energy waste by turning off lights and computers when you are not in the room or using the computer.

Geothermal Uses

People like to take advantage of Earth's heat where hot water makes pools. Water that is underground in geothermal reservoirs can be used directly in industry and to heat homes and businesses. A well is tapped into the geothermal reservoir, and a system of pipes and mechanical pumps delivers the heated water to the surface. The used water is then returned back to the well. These methods of using geothermal energy save on the amount of fossil fuels used for heat.

Swimmers enjoy the warm, clean water of Iceland's Blue Lagoon. The lagoon was created by water from the power plant in the background, where water is pumped from one mile (1.6 km) below the surface.

Hot Springs and Spas

Hot springs form where geothermally heated groundwater reaches the surface. These warm outdoor springs are found in even the coldest climates. The warmest hot springs are in volcanic regions, such as in Japan. In Japan, hot-spring baths are called *onsen*, and the tradition of hot-spring bathing is hundreds of years old. In Beppu, a city in southern Japan, there are nearly 4,000 hot springs. About 12 million tourists visit the city's *onsens* each year. Many people believe the waters of hot springs have **therapeutic** powers because of the high mineral content in the water. Hot water can hold dissolved minerals. Resorts called **spas** are often built close to hot springs.

Community Heating

By tapping into reservoirs of a temperature of 140°F (60°C) or hotter, homes and other buildings in a community can be heated using geothermal energy. In a geothermal-heating system for an entire district or area, a well is drilled to reach the reservoir. The hot water is pumped through a **heat exchanger**.

Heat Exchanger

In a heat exchanger, the pipes carrying geothermal water come into contact with pipes carrying city water. The heat transfers from the heated pipes to the city-water pipes. The heated city water is then piped to buildings, where it heats the air. Geothermal district-heating systems are used in France, the United States, Turkey, Poland, Hungary, China, and Japan. The world's largest system is in Reykjavik, Iceland, where almost all buildings are heated this way.

CASE STUDY

Klamath Falls, Oregon

Klamath Falls, Oregon, has one of the largest geothermal district-heating systems in the United States. The production wells lie just outside the city, and a one-mile (1.6-km) pipe transfers water to the heat-exchange facility in town. There, city water is heated, and the geothermal water is returned to the reservoir through an injector well. The heated city water is then pumped to two heat exchangers in city buildings. The city also heats some of its downtown sidewalks using geothermal energy. Pipes buried under the sidewalks carry heat that melts the snow in winter.

Almost two miles (about 3 km) of pipes buried under the city supplies heated water to 24 buildings and four greenhouses.

Hot Crops!

Geothermal energy is also used in agriculture and other industries. It is used worldwide to boost agriculture production, especially in the United States and Iceland. In places where the climate is **temperate**, or cooler, crops can be **irrigated** with warm geothermal water. Spraying hot water on fields also **sterilizes** the soil, helping prevent pests and crop disease. Geothermal hot water pumped under the soil in pipes heats the soil and produces better crops and a longer growing season. Geothermal energy is also used to help heat greenhouses. Greenhouses trap the Sun's heat but also require a lot of additional heat to operate. Geothermally heated water is used to warm the air and the soil in the greenhouses. Some farmers estimate that geothermal energy reduces 80 percent of their fuel costs for their greenhouses.

Conservation Tip

When doing laundry, use cold water instead of warm or hot water. You will save the energy needed to heat the water.

Other Uses

Geothermal energy is also used in some industries and in **aquaculture**. Aquaculture is farming fish and other water animals and plants for sale. Usually, fish and other animals grow slowly during cooler seasons. Geothermal energy keeps the water warm year-round, so the animals mature faster. Geothermal aquaculture is used in China to raise fish and shrimp, in Japan to raise eels and alligators, and in the western United States to raise alligators and different types of fish. Some companies that dry food, do laundry, mine for gold, manufacture paper, or dye cloth also use geothermal energy.

Geothermal Heat Pumps

Buildings can also be heated without a geothermal reservoir. **Geothermal heat pumps** (GHPs) are a system of underground pipes connected to a heat pump that use Earth's heat to warm buildings. The deeper down into the Earth you dig, the hotter the temperature. This heat comes not only from Earth's inner heat, but also from solar energy that is trapped in the ground. The pipes of the GHP system are buried in a loop deep under ground, beside or underneath a building. That far under ground, the temperature remains at an almost constant 45°F to 75°F (7°C to 24°C). Earth heats a liquid inside the pipes, which then goes to the building. This system is also used for cooling during the summer. The liquid in the pipes absorbs the heat from buildings in summer and transfers it back into the ground. As an added bonus, the system provides free hot water during the summer.

Aurora Ice Museum, Alaska

In Fairbanks, Alaska, geothermal energy is used to keep an ice hotel open year-round. The hotel, called the Aurora Ice Museum, is made out of ice and snow. It includes a great hall and lounge, ice sculptures, and even chandeliers made from ice. In summer, temperatures in Fairbanks can rise to 90°F (32°C), which is warm enough to cause the hotel to start to melt. To keep the hotel cool without having to pay for expensive electricity, a device called an absorption chiller uses heat to provide electricity for cooling. The heat comes from geothermal energy.

Over 1,000 tons of ice and snow were used to create the Aurora Ice Museum.

Power Plants

Geothermal energy can also be used to **generate** electricity in thermal power plants. There are three types of geothermal power plants: **dry steam**, **flash**, and **binary**. In a geothermal power plant, steam or hot water from reservoirs is used to create electricity.

Dry-Steam Power Plants

Dry-steam power plants are built where there are steam fields. Steam fields are very rare.

They occur where water that has been heated by magma is trapped under rock and turns to steam. Wells are drilled through the rock to reach the steam. The steam is piped to the surface, where it is used to drive turbines and power generators in dry-steam power plants. The used steam **condenses** to water that is pumped back into the reservoir to be heated again. There are only a few places in the world where power plants like this can be built.

Generating Electricity

To generate electricity, thermal power plants convert the moving energy in a gas or liquid into electricity. Most power plants today burn coal to make steam to power the turbine blades. Instead of using coal as an energy source, geothermal power plants use Earth's heat.

1. Steam powers the blades of a turbine.
2. The turning blades cause the shaft to rotate.
3. The shaft leads to a generator, where it is surrounded by coiled wires. When the shaft rotates, the wires create an **electromagnet**, which produces an electric current.
4. The electric current, or electricity, is sent to homes and businesses.

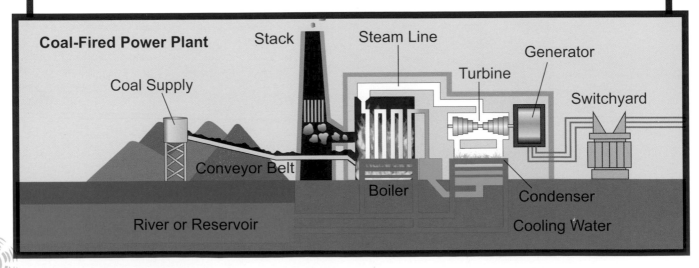

The Geysers, California

The Geysers is a steam field in northern California. There are 21 dry-steam power plants in operation at The Geysers. Power production started there in 1960. By 1987, it supplied 1.8 million people in the area with electricity. Today, The Geysers provides one million households with power. The operators at The Geysers have learned important lessons about sustaining steam fields. A lot of steam is lost through evaporation at the power plants' cooling towers. To make sure the resource will not be used up, reclaimed wastewater from local areas is piped to The Geysers and under ground into the steam fields to be heated.

California produces the most geothermal electricity out of all the U.S. states. The geothermal power plants of California produce almost half of the world's geothermally-generated electricity. The City of San Bernardino heats almost 40 buildings.

Flash-Steam Plants

The most common type of geothermal power plant today is the flash-steam plant. Flash-steam plants use water that is between 360°F and 700°F (182°C and 371°C). Water usually boils and starts to turn to water vapor at 212°F (100°C). Sometimes, it can be heated deep below the surface past its boiling point without turning to steam. Instead, the water keeps getting hotter and hotter until it becomes super heated. The super-heated water is pumped to the surface. It is sprayed into a low-**pressure** flash tank, where some of the water rapidly 'flashes,' or turns to steam. The steam powers the turbine in the power plant, and the remaining water is returned to the well.

Binary Power Plants

In binary power plants, geothermal energy is transferred to a secondary, or binary, liquid. The binary liquid has a much lower boiling point than water does, which means it needs less heat to produce steam. Examples of binary fluids are isobutane and isopentane. Binary power plants work with lower-temperature water reservoirs. The temperature is between 100°F and 300°F (38°C and 148°C). Wells drilled into the reservoir bring the warm water to the surface, where it passes through a heat exchanger. In the heat exchanger, the binary liquid is heated and moved to a separate tank to be flashed to steam. After driving the turbine, the binary liquid is cooled and reused.

Conservation Tip

To use less electricity, turn off computers, televisions, DVD players, and video-game players every time you finish using them.

This geothermal facility at Mammoth Lake,
California, produces clean electricity in
an environmentally friendly manner.

Geothermal History

Geothermal energy has only been used to generate electricity for just over 100 years. Using geothermal energy directly has a much longer history.

Sacred Springs

Native North Americans used hot springs in the Southwestern United States for hundreds of years before Europeans arrived. The hot springs were believed to have healing powers. Warring Native nations never fought at the hot springs in Calistoga, California, because they believed the area around the hot springs was sacred, or holy. The Wappo Indians built sweat lodges for ceremonies over the steam escaping from **fumaroles**. A fumarole is a small hole or vent in the ground through which steam or other gases escape.

Healing Baths

Balneology is the science of using natural mineral-spring water for healing. Some people believe that spring water was used for healing in Asia as far back as 5,000 years ago. In Japan, *onsens*, or hot springs, are an important part of the culture. The hot springs are used for healing. This healing power is derived from the minerals dissolved in the hot water. An inn called a *ryokan* was sometimes built around hot springs. Japan's military leaders, called *shoguns*, liked to visit them to enjoy hot-spring baths. There were separate communal baths for men and women. A good soak in an *onsen* relieves aches, pains, and diseases.

Women soak in a Japanese communal hot spring, called an onsen. *The* onsen *is said to be good for a person's health.*

Larderello, Italy

In Tuscany, Italy, hot springs have been used since Roman times. In 1904, an Italian scientist named Prince Piero Ginori Conti demonstrated that geothermal energy could be used to generate electricity when he used steam to power light bulbs. In 1913, in an area known as 'Devil's Valley,' because of all the steam escaping from vents in the ground, the first geothermal power plant was built. By 1943, the dry steam plant at Larderello was making electricity for 130,000 homes. It was completely destroyed during World War II and rebuilt. Today, the Larderello power plant continues to produce electricity.

Romans

The ancient Romans also used geothermal energy for hot-spring bathing, spas, and for treating eye and skin diseases. In Pompeii, a city in what is now southeastern Italy, geothermal hot water was piped into homes for heating. Pompeii was built in the shadow of a volcano called Mount Vesuvius. This volcano erupted, destroying the city and killing all its inhabitants in 79 A.D. When the ancient Romans expanded their empire, they spread the custom of public bathing. In 43 A.D., the Romans invaded England and found the only naturally occurring hot spring in that country. There, they built a temple and public bath. Today, this is the city of Bath.

Powering the West

In the United States, the use of geothermal energy was already popular before the first power plant was built there in 1921. In Boise, Idaho, the United States' first district-heating system was set up in 1892. It piped hot water from nearby hot springs into town to heat homes and businesses. By 1852, a spa had been built at The Geysers in California. Famous Americans, such as author Mark Twain and President Theodore Roosevelt, visited. When John D. Grant built the first U.S. geothermal power plant, it was to produce power for a resort at The Geysers. In 1960, the Pacific Gas and Electric Company expanded electricity production at The Geysers.

The Maori, an aboriginal group in New Zealand, traditionally used hot springs as a heat source for cooking.

Oil Crisis

Despite the advances in geothermal energy, fossil fuels were the cheapest and most plentiful energy source. During the 1970s, fossil fuels met many countries' needs for electricity. In 1973, however, there was a shortage of oil in North America, Japan, and Europe. Governments began to investigate alternative energy sources, including geothermal energy. When fossil fuels became more available again in the 1980s, geothermal research funding from governments declined along with people's interest in the energy. Today, people are more aware of the environmental damage caused by burning fossil fuels. Interest in geothermal energy has been sparked once more.

During the oil crisis of the 1970s, many service stations ran out of gasoline to sell. The shortage was a result of some oil-producing countries refusing to sell oil to Europe, North America, and Japan.

Conservation Tip

Many containers and materials can be recycled today. It is easy to determine whether a product is recyclable. Many plastics have a recycling code on the product's container. Products made from recycled materials are also usually clearly marked on the outside so that consumers can know they are buying materials that used less energy and fewer resources to produce.

The Great Debate

All energy sources have benefits and drawbacks. Alternative energy sources are less harmful to the environment than fossil fuels are, but they are not perfect. Solar and wind power, for example, are **intermittent**. This means they only work when the sun is shining or when the wind is blowing. Using geothermal power plants, on the other hand, generates electricity 98 percent of the time.

The Cost

One of the biggest drawbacks to using geothermal power is the amount of time and money required to find a suitable place to tap into Earth's heat. Before a geothermal power plant can be set up, wells have to be drilled into reservoirs. Some reservoirs are close to the surface, but others are buried very deep. First, **geologists** analyze maps and other data to determine if a spot is suitable for a well. Then, a deep, narrow hole is drilled to obtain a rock sample, which is tested. If the test shows that the site can produce geothermal power, a production well is drilled. The cost of digging the production well can be one million dollars or more. The new geothermal power plant must be built directly over the well because steam cannot be transported over long distances. It loses heat over distances. Many geothermal power plants are in remote areas. Miles of expensive power lines have to be built and maintained so the electricity will reach consumers. Once geothermal plants have been built, they are inexpensive to maintain and last for many years.

Large rigs are used to drill production wells. The wells can be over two miles (3 km) deep.

24

The Guarantee

One benefit to geothermal power is that once a geothermal plant is up and running, the cost of electricity will remain at a constant price. Unlike fossil fuels, this energy source is not bought and sold and does not have to be brought in from other countries. Geothermal power plants are also not affected by weather or disasters. A properly managed geothermal power plant runs 24 hours a day, seven days a week.

Emissions

Geothermal energy is a green energy source. The most significant emission released is water vapor. Dry-steam and flash-steam power plants also release small amounts of carbon dioxide, nitric oxide, and sulfur. They release much less carbon dioxide than coal-burning power plants do. Sulfur is a gas that makes the area around the power plants smell like rotten eggs. Binary power plants produce no emissions.

Many people in North America and in Europe are working to decrease their dependence on foreign oil supplies.

Kenya, Africa

Many places in Africa are potential sites for geothermal power production. In Kenya, a country in eastern Africa, the Olkaria geothermal power plant has been operating since the 1980s. It is the largest power plant of its kind in Africa. Currently, only about 15 percent of Kenyans have electricity. By expanding geothermal-energy production, it is estimated that geothermal power can supply all of Kenya's 34 million people with electricity. Unfortunately, the country does not have the money to make this happen.

The Great Rift Valley runs through Kenya. It formed millions of years ago where Earth's crust broke apart. Magma is close to Earth's surface in the Great Rift Valley, so the possibility of harnessing geothermal energy in the area is high.

Resource Management

Geothermal power plants use water. Earth's heat is always available, but the water must be properly managed. Once the water has been used, it is returned to the ground. Some water escapes into the air as water vapor. In some places, including California, reclaimed wastewater is used to replenish the reservoir. Geothermal power plants require less land than other types of power plants do, but each plant is smaller, and many wells have to be drilled. In some areas, people are concerned that the land around geothermal power plants will start to sink if too much water or steam is taken from the ground.

The illustration (right) shows the design of a typical geothermal power plant. Wells are dug deep into the ground to tap into the heat below the surface.

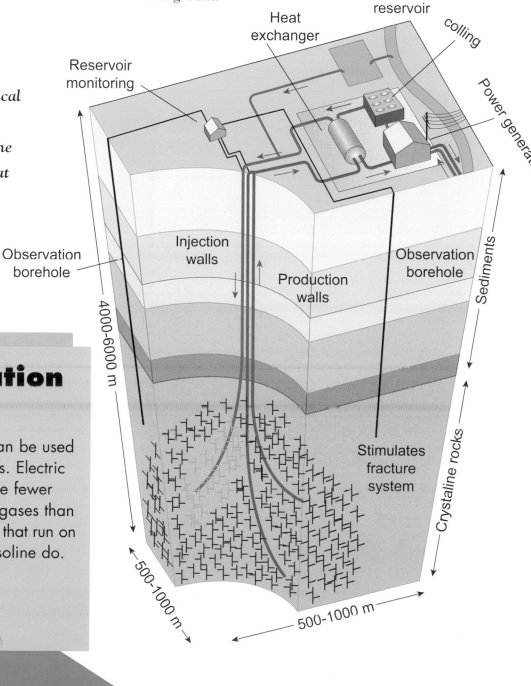

Conservation Tip

Geothermal energy can be used to power electric cars. Electric cars release fewer waste gases than cars that run on gasoline do.

27

Future Energy

Making geothermal energy a main energy source in the future will take major investments in time and money. Technology needs to be developed, and people need to be educated. In the meantime, people around the world, especially in industrialized countries such as the United States, Canada, China, and the countries of Europe, can do a lot to lessen the amount of energy they use every day.

Incentives

Today, about 9,000 megawatts of geothermal electricity is produced in 21 countries around the world. The United States is the biggest producer of geothermal energy. Competition from other energy sources and recent cuts in government funding may halt the development of geothermal electricity. In some countries, governments give incentives, such as **rebates**, to encourage people and businesses to use alternative energy sources. An incentive is a reward for doing something.

Alternative Sources

Some U.S. states require electric companies to produce a specified amount of electricity from alternative sources. For Western states, geothermal energy is a good option. Energy experts believe that there is tremendous potential for geothermal power there. They estimate that Montana, for example, has more than 25,000 square miles (64,750 km²) of potential sites.

Conservation Tip

In summer, raise the air-conditioner temperature setting a few degrees. In winter, lower the heat temperature setting of your furnace a few degrees. You probably will not notice the difference, but you will be saving energy.

Tapping Sites

Some sites are better suited than others for tapping into Earth's heat. Finding the best sites is expensive. New technology is being developed to better evaluate sites before drilling. These technologies include better modeling tools for computers and better drills that allow for deeper wells. At sites where geothermal energy is deep below the surface, wells will have to be dug deeper. Most rock 5 to 10 miles (8 to 16 km) below the surface is hot enough to create electricity. By pumping water into the wells to create a reservoir, geothermal energy can be brought to the surface. Using this "hot rock" system, geothermal energy can be tapped anywhere on Earth.

A Geothermal Town

Over half the population of Iceland lives in the capital city of Reykjavik. It was once one of the world's most polluted cities. Today, Reykjavik is one of the cleanest, thanks to the city's geothermal district-heating system. In 1930, the first geothermal district-heating system was used to heat a school. Soon after, other buildings were added to the system. Ninety percent of all homes in the country are now heated by geothermal energy. Iceland has no oil reserves of its own, so the only oil it buys from other countries is used in transportation. In addition, most of its electricity is created through hydropower.

In Iceland, steam is used to produce heat and electricity in large geothermal power plants, which is then transported to houses and other buildings.

BORHOLA NJ 11
BORAR 1985, HOLUDYPI 2265m
H.Y.S. 187.3m

Timeline

(above) *Health spas were traditionally located on the sites of hot springs.*

(below) *Volcanoes release geothermal energy in the form of lava.*

Geothermal energy has been used worldwide for many years. It is one of the oldest energy sources. Here are some important dates in the history of geothermal energy.

1500 B.C.

Ancient Romans, Japanese, and Chinese use hot springs for bathing, cooking, and heating.

1100 B.C.

Coal may have been used as fuel.

1847

William Bell Elliot finds a steaming valley just north of San Francisco, California. Elliot calls the area The Geysers and thinks he has found the gates of Hell.

1886

In Banff, Alberta, Canada, hot-spring water is piped to a hotel and spa.

1892

The United States' first geothermal district-heating system is established in Boise, Idaho.

1913

Italian scientist Piero Ginori Conti invents the first geothermal electric power plant in Larderello, Italy.

1919

The first geothermal wells in Japan are drilled at Beppu.

1928

Iceland begins using geothermally heated water for district heating.

1958

A geothermal flash-steam power plant begins operating in New Zealand.

1960

Pacific Gas and Electric begins operating the first large-scale geothermal power plant at The Geysers.

1972

Deep-well-drilling technology improves.

1973

Oil crisis begins, and governments sponsor renewable-energy research programs in Germany, Sweden, Canada, the United Kingdom, and the United States.

1977

The first hot "dry rock" reservoir is developed at Fenton Hill, New Mexico.

1995

Worldwide geothermal capacity reaches 6,000 megawatts.

2000

The Unites States Department of Energy begins a program to determine the possibility of developing geothermal energy in the West. Over 8,000 megawatts of electricity and over 15,000 megawatts of thermal energy are being produced from geothermal sources worldwide.

2005

The U.S. *Energy Policy Act* gives federal tax credits to new geothermal power plants, thus encouraging the use of geothermal power. Twenty-four countries around the world report generating 8,900 megawatts of electricity through geothermal power plants. Seventy-two countries are using geothermal energy.

2007

Fifteen countries, including the United States and Mexico, join the International Energy Agency (IEA) for international cooperation in geothermal research and development.

Geothermal power plants in Iceland produce enough energy to support the energy requirements of many of its cities.

Glossary

atmosphere The layers of gases that surround Earth. Some of these gases are nitrogen, oxygen, carbon dioxide, and water vapor

biomass Organic, or once living, matter that can be used as a fuel source. Some examples of biomass include corn, wood chips, and animal waste

condense To cause a gas to turn into a liquid

consumption The act of using something

convection The movement of a fluid where the warmer portions rise and the colder portions sink; also the transfer of heat in a liquid or gas

cooling towers Large towers that let off the heat from cooling liquids at a power plant

electromagnet A magnet produced by electricity

energy efficient Describes a machine that uses less energy to do the same amount of work as another machine

environment The air, water, soil, and all things around us

generate To create or produce

geologist A scientist who studies rocks and minerals to find out what Earth is made of and the changes on its surface

greenhouses Buildings enclosed in glass or plastic where plants are grown

irrigate To supply land with water through channels, pipes, or streams

pressure The amount of weight, usually air, pushing down on something. Low pressure means there is little air. High pressure means there is a lot of air

radioactive Giving off energy in the form of rays. Being near radioactive material can make a person very ill

rebate The return of part of a payment

reclaimed wastewater Sewer water that has been treated, or cleaned, and is ready to be used for another purpose

replenish To fill something that was empty

reserve Something that is saved for future use

silt Fine dirt

sterilize To get rid of dirt or germs

therapeutic Having to do with the treatment of disease or illness

turbine An engine that is run by a stream of liquid or gas that moves against its blades and turns them

water vapor Water in the form of a gas

work The force on an object and the distance it is moved

Index

Printed in the U.S.A.